THE EAST ANGLIA
COLOURING BOOK

First published 2016

The History Press
The Mill, Brimscombe Port
Stroud, Gloucestershire, GL5 2QG
www.thehistorypress.co.uk

British Library Cataloguing in Publication Data.
A catalogue record for this book is available from the British Library.

ISBN 978 0 7509 6802 7

Cover colouring by Lucy Hester.
Typesetting and origination by The History Press
Printed in Great Britain

THE EAST ANGLIA

COLOURING BOOK

PAST AND PRESENT

Take some time out of your busy life to relax and unwind with this feel–good colouring book designed for everyone who loves East Anglia.

Absorb yourself in the simple action of colouring in the scenes and settings from around the region of East Anglia, past and present. From iconic architecture to picturesque coastal vistas, you are sure to find some of your favourite locations waiting to be transformed with a splash of colour. Bring these scenes alive as you de-stress with this inspiring and calming colouring book.

There are no rules – choose any page and any choice of colouring pens or pencils you like to create your own unique, colourful and creative illustrations.

The entrance to Clacton pier, Essex ▸

Houghton Mill (National Trust), Cambridgeshire ▸

Ipswich marina, Suffolk ▸

Thetford Forest, Norfolk ▸

Nene Valley Railway, Peterborough, Cambridgeshire ▸

Audley End House, Saffron Walden, Essex ▶

Hemingford Grey, Cambridgeshire, *c.* 1900 ▸

Wivenhoe, Essex ▸

Trinity College, Cambridge, Cambridgeshire ▸

Seals on Blakeney Point, Norfolk ▶

Denham Lock, Grand Union Canal, Essex ▶

Beth Chatto Gardens, Colchester, Essex ▸

Mundesley-on-Sea, Norfolk, 1890s ▸

East Anglia Transport Museum, Suffolk ▶

Norwich Cathedral cloisters, Norfolk ▸

Wolf at Colchester Zoo, Essex ▶

St Ives, Cambridgeshire ▸

Museum of East Anglia Life, Stowmarket, Suffolk ▸

Adventure Island, Southend-on-Sea, Essex ▸

Ely Cathedral, Cambridgeshire ▸

Norwich Castle, Norfolk ▸

St Neots, Cambridgeshire ▶

Waltham Abbey, *c.* 1930 ▸

Bourne Mill, Colchester, Essex ▸

Christchurch Mansion & Wolsey Art Gallery, Ipswich, Suffolk ▸

Great Yarmouth beach huts, Norfolk ▸

Orford Castle, Suffolk ▸

The Fitzwilliam Museum, Cambridge, Cambridgeshire ▸

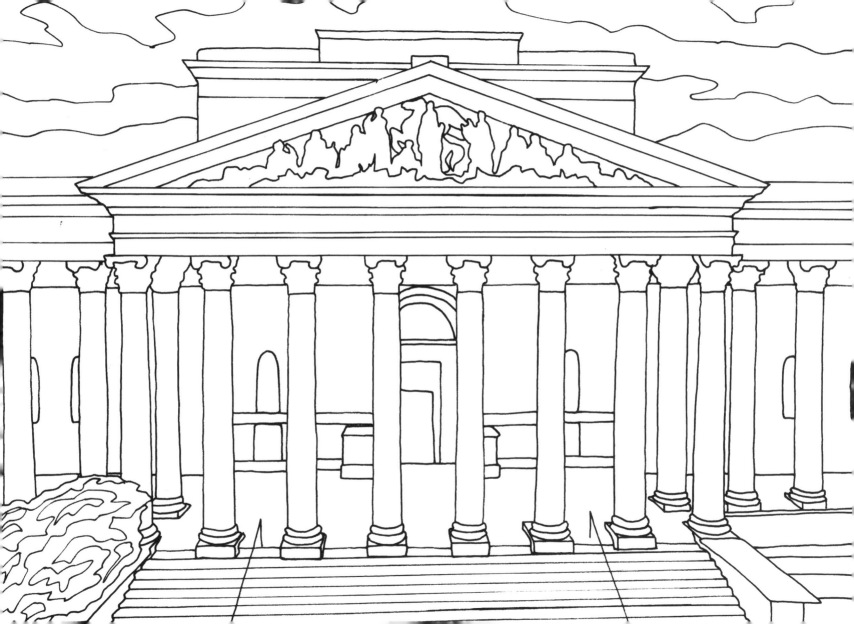

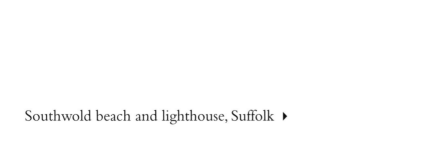

Southwold beach and lighthouse, Suffolk ▸

Wimpole Estate, Arrington, Cambridgeshire ▸

Hickling Staithe and Pleasure Boat Inn, Norfolk , *c.* 1900 ▸

Wicken Windmill, Cambridgeshire ▸

Chelmsford, Essex, *c.* 1950 ▸

Framlingham Castle, Suffolk ▸

West Cliff, Cromer, Norfolk, *c.* 1950 ▸

Flatford Mill, East Bergholt, Suffolk ▸

Sandringham House, Norfolk ▸

Newmarket High Street with racehorses on
the way to the racecourse, Suffolk, *c.* 1900 ▸

Oliver Cromwell's House, Ely, Cambridgeshire ▸

Norfolk Broads, Norfolk ▸

King's College Chapel, Cambridge, Cambridgeshire ▸

Abbey Gardens, Bury St Edmunds, Suffolk ▸

Holt, Norfolk ▸

Pigs at Jimmy's Farm, Ipswich, Suffolk ▶

Bridge of Sighs, Cambridge, Cambridgeshire ▸

Also from The History Press

THE ESSEX
COLOURING BOOK

PAST AND PRESENT